EFFECTIVE LEADERS:

MENTOR PEOPLE &

MANAGE PROCESSES

To God be the Glory

I give all honor to God who strengthens me and provides me with knowledge and direction. I thank you Lord for allowing me to reach others in a way that is unique and informative. Thank you for giving me the gifts, talents, and the ability to lead others and get results. All I do and all I will ever do is magnify You.

NIV, Romans 12:5-8

> *We have different gifts, according to the grace given us. If a man's gift is prophesying, let him use it in proportion to his faith. If it is serving, let him serve; if it is teaching, let him teach; if it is encouraging, let him encourage; if it is contributing to the needs of others, let him give generously; if it is leadership, let him govern diligently; if it is showing mercy, let him do it cheerfully.*

Thank You

I thank my wonderful wife Jeannett for buffering and supporting me. This is our work. This is our accomplishment because without you, I would be without my soul. I appreciate the talks and feedback you provide when I discuss work and personal issues with you. I know you think I don't listen but your voice is in every thought and decision I make.

He who finds a wife finds what is good
and receives favor from the LORD.

(NIV, Proverbs 18:22)

I thank God for my children – Being a father is the most difficult and wonderful job in the world. I was not there for all of you, but I did the best with what I knew how to do. As God has made me a better man, I became a better father. I thank God that you are all healthy. No questions:

Lemar, Janelle, Sasha, Malcolm, Jenae

My Parents are Phenomenal – They gave and give their best – I thank God for allowing me 50 years with my parents and counting. I know everyone doesn't get that Blessing and I am truly grateful. Thank You God!

James & Theresa
John & Patricia

My brothers and sisters, you are all remarkable and you have all planted a seed in me to make me who I am today: Thank You!

Kim, Sabrina, Louis, Todd, Malik
Donna, Tondia, Jr., Cola

A special thank you to my Cathedral & CORE Church Family – You do not realize the impact you have had and continue to have on my life. Thank You

Thank you to those who submitted letters! I still need more for future volumes so hmu

About the Author

James Sutton Jr. is the current Campus President at Virginia College in Macon, GA. James has over 30 years' experience in Recruitment, Management and Personal Development. He has conducted dozens of workshops to motivate and encourage others to succeed. His first book, "Look at Your Boss! Rehabilitation for Your Career," was well received by his target audience of young adults to inspire them to finish school, get training, and not settle for their current place in life.

James is a 23 year retired United States Air Force and Marine Corps Veteran and the recipient of 'The Airman's Medal' for Heroism.

James is a licensed Minister of the Gospel under the tutelage of Bishop Waylyn Hobbs Jr., Senior Pastor of Coney Island Cathedral of Deliverance, Brooklyn, NY.

He also served as an Elder at CORE Church, Mount Holly, NC - Pastor Tim McCarn is Senior Pastor.

Inspire Leadership Potential:

The best leader is the one who has sense enough to pick good 'people' to do what he wants done, and the self-restraint to keep from meddling with them while they do it.

~Theodore Roosevelt, American President

A genuine leader is not a searcher for consensus but a molder of consensus.

~ Martin Luther King, Jr.

Effective leadership is not about making speeches or being liked; leadership is defined by results not attributes.

~Peter Drucker

Leadership cannot really be taught. It can only be learned.

~ Harold S. Geneen

Leaders must be close enough to relate to others, but far enough ahead to motivate them.

~ John C. Maxwell

MSG 1 Timothy 3:1-7

Leadership in the Church

If anyone wants to provide leadership in the church, good! But there are preconditions: A leader must be well-thought-of, committed to his wife, cool and collected, accessible, and hospitable. He must know what he's talking about, not be over fond of wine, not pushy but gentle, not thin-skinned, not money-hungry. He must handle his own affairs well, attentive to his own children and having their respect. For if someone is unable to handle his own affairs, how can he take care of God's church? He must not be a new believer, lest the position go to his head and the Devil trip him up. Outsiders must think well of him, or else the Devil will figure out a way to lure him into his trap.

Table of Contents

Effective Leaders

Mentor People & Manage Processes

Management is a Science - Leadership is an Art

Leadership and Management must be studied and then applied to be effective. Everyone has the gift of leadership and the ability to lead!

"What are you talking about James, that's not true?"
Says the Inner Voice

It is true – You may doubt that statement but everyone can lead! The distinction between an effective and ineffective leader is that some leaders have natural leadership ability – and other leaders must study, rehearse, and practice to perfect their leadership skills. It may take time for the unnatural leader to make leadership appear or become more natural. We have all witnessed novice leaders at work. We watched as some evolved to become effective leaders and we saw others flop. Personally, I have had a variety of effective and ineffective leaders, nerdy leaders, cool leaders, bad leaders, church leaders, good leaders, soft leaders, hard leaders, effective leaders, and ineffective leaders.

"What do you mean by bad leaders James?" Says
the Inner Voice

The one thing I have found is ineffective and bad leaders have one thing in common... well maybe a few things. They attempted to manage people with ineffective processes. Often time, the job was accomplished but every new project had the same negative overtone; which made for a horrible work environment... extremely horrible.

This book will not go through all the theory of management vs. leadership – We won't discuss styles, pro & cons, what works best... etc. etc. etc. –It is simpler than that. This is a book about your mindset and approach to leadership. This book won't ask you the question "Blanchard or Hersy?"

"James, you can't simplify leadership"
Says the Inner Voice

I beg to differ; I have seen some good managers try to apply the learned leadership styles that didn't fit their personality. – They would try to mimic their mentors and predecessor; that does not work. Leadership is about finding out who you are and applying it accordingly. You can't just try to fit in... some try to get a triangle to fit in a square. Situational leadership isn't about applying the same leadership style to a unique situation.

"What that look like James..."says the Inner Voice

A hot mess! I can go on...

"that don't work" says the Inner Voice

I've seen leaders attempt to fit workers into a cookie cutter unorganized process. They give passionate speeches about nothing to try to get the unorganized process to work. However, the speeches wouldn't inspire an ant to pick up a crumb of bread because the process is broke.

"Wow, lol... I know, Mentor People and Manage Processes, right James?" says the inner voice

Right, inner voice – Look, for some of you; this is not your first book on leadership development; however, it will be one of the shortest and straight to the point books you will ever read. You can add the volumes that are relevant to your situation. I know most books talk about the differences between management and leadership; I won't – Think about it, the goal of effective management is to produce and to be a good leader. –The goal of effective leadership is to motivate people into action...

"But, how?" says the inner voice

If this is your first book on becoming an effective leader, you picked the right one.

"Sounds a little biased James" says the inner voice

– Look inner voice, I am going to give it to you straight. If you need the theory, the charts, and graphs, get another book; chances are you may not be leadership material. You might make a good manager. Just saying – The charts and graphs fall under the management processes – effective leaders empower and drive people to success by mentoring, encouraging, and motivating!

> *"James, in your other book, Look at Your Boss; Rehabilitation of Your Career, you said you did not believe in Mentors" says the inner voice*

Don't twist my words, inner voice. What I said was… Mentors had to want to mentor, get it right. As a leader you have to be willing to inspire your people to the next level.

Hey, before we start arguing, let's dig into the book. I am open to discussion but as you read this book, think about some of your former leaders that have been successful. Not the T.V. folk that just report the good news.

I'm talking about the leaders you connected with that made you work. You appreciated their input; you welcomed it – You knew they had your best interest at heart – You appreciated the fact that you were given a clear vision to work with each day. The direction and vision didn't change every other day. It didn't change every time the leader made a new connection or when the leader was met with the challenge to produce. They mentored people and managed the process. They didn't force people to work, they inspired people to work. Effective leaders follow through and follow up. Did I mention that they mentored people and managed processes - Effective Leaders don't teach work ethic!

Managers push work ethic, they drive work ethic, and adjust or try to mentor the process to account for the poor work ethic – they drive their workers in the ground instead of holding them accountable with inspiration and motivation - Their constant grinding technique of managing puts an undue burden on the team. If you are spending your time teaching work ethic and driving your people without challenging their poor work ethic, you burden the team and they feel the stress and the pressure of ineffective leadership.

"James, that's not always the case"
Says the inner voice

Really? Look at any ineffective team. Those that are not holding up their end of the bargain… How many times have you been a part of a dysfunctional team?

Every time you start a new project, it seems like it's the first time; this happens even when there is a process in place and the task is repetitive. Why?

But you will see as you turn the pages of this book and really dig in; I will give some examples of my experiences as a Leader. I am far from perfect but leadership is not about you being perfect – It's about you effectively reaching for perfection. Leaders with an effective process, with people ready to be coached, can be successful without the added burden and stress that come with management.

Throughout the book, I will share letters from my current and former supervises, employees, and business associates as a testimony of how effective leadership can make you feel.

My final thought before we jump in:

This book is for you – The aspiring leader – The leader that wants an innovative way to lead without all the "muckerdy muck" as one of my great leaders Elaine would say. This book is not about me, although it could be one heck of a long resume. We will move forward transparent, with the hope of showing you that leadership ability is about connecting with the people you are leading. Management is about understanding and perfecting processes.

Professional Reference #1:

James Sutton Jr. is a person of extraordinary character and virtue. I met Mr. Sutton during his tenure with ITT Technical Institute. In our initial meeting James's leadership abilities surpassed anything I could have imagined. He was very knowledgeable about various topics, and offered his assistance immediately.

James challenged me to be a better coach, by becoming somewhat of a mentor to me. He was a massive resource for ideas and encouragement. Mr. Sutton utilized his leadership abilities to coordinate events and he introduced me to several reputable people. He utilized his leadership role most recently to introduce me to the Virginia College staff. They then invited me to make the commencement speech for their graduating class.

Mr. James Sutton has been an influential leader in my life. Leaders are supposed to empower, and inspire you to be a better person. Mr. Sutton has influenced me to do just that.

Demetra Moore Author, CPC, ELI-MP
"Moore Out of Life"

Keynote Speaker

James Sutton Jr.

March 22, 2013

The National Society of Leadership and Success
– Sigma Alpha Pi –

Dr. O'Dea, Dean Duerr, Miss Ward, Faculty, Students, and Honored guest... and members and future inductees to Sigma Alpha Pi

I thank you for allowing me to be your Speaker this afternoon for the Virginia College Spartanburg Chapter Induction ceremony!

I won't be before you very long, just long enough to tell you about 4 people – we all know them as...

Everybody, Somebody, Anybody, and Nobody. You may have heard this story about these four people but I want to share it with you once more; to provide you some guidance as you embark on your journey of leadership and success. Here goes...

"There was an important job to be done and Everybody was asked to do it. Everybody was sure Somebody would do it. Anybody could have done it, but Nobody did it. Somebody got angry about that, because it was Everybody's job. Everybody thought Anybody could do it but Nobody realized that Everybody wouldn't do it. It ended up that Everybody blamed Somebody when Nobody did what Anybody could have done."

Leadership is about getting it done! And yes Anybody can do it! But Everybody won't-

Harold Geneen shares, Leadership cannot really be taught. It can only be learned.

I agree; And Somebody has to be willing to learn...

The mission statement of The National Society of Leadership and Success states, "it's a community where like-minded success oriented individuals come together and help one another succeed."

Like-minded success driven people – somebodies working together so nobody gets left behind!

Leadership can't be taught – you have to want to learn to lead. You have to want to be the Somebody that gets it done – Mark Twain stated Thunder is impressive, but it is lightning that does the work.

It amazes me how many people get excited with a little rumbling in the sky - I want to see the light!

The National Society of Leadership and Success mission statement also says it serves as a powerful force of good in the greater community by encouraging and organizing action to better the world.

The Greater Community??? – You are tasked with doing well for the greater community - You are being tasked to better the world. "Sigma Alpha PI"

I saw a sign in a Restaurant window that read... Don't stand there and be hungry; come on in and get fed!

As leaders you have to want to be fed – You have to come in and get fed! Nobody can want it more than you! Somebody has to reach out and get some – Everybody has the ability to get it – but a leader can't just be anybody! Leadership can't be taught it can only be learned!

I read a sign at a Car Dealership that said-
The best way to get back on your feet: miss a car payment.

If I wanted to get on my feet, I would stand up – But leaders understand that sometimes it takes the unconventional road to make things happen... leaders find a way to motivate people to stand in the midst of adversity – Now I am not advising anyone here to miss a car payment but I want to encourage you as a leader to be hungry, and to come inside and get fed.

The National Society of Leadership and Success wants to know "Are they helping as many people as the can in the greatest way possible?" They say they are dream supporters – that build leaders, supports people to accomplish their dreams, and they better the world in the process. They get people to ask one important question -- 'What would you do if you knew you couldn't fail?' and then they help them to achieve those goals."

Inductees, I want to encourage you today!!! - So I will leave you with one very important nugget! ~ hear me! Don't let your yesterday use up too much of your today. Somebody didn't get that... so I will say it again... Do not let your yesterday take up too much of your today. Nobody will do you better than you.

I remember one night I came back to work. Not a soul was in the office except a big dog emptying wastebaskets. Now I stared at the animal, wondering if my imagination... my mind was playing tricks on me. The dog looked up and said, "Don't be surprised. This is just part of my job." "Wow, Incredible!" I said. "I can't believe it! Does your boss know what a prize he has in you? An animal that can talk!" "No, no," pleaded the dog. "Please don't tell him! If that man finds out I can talk, he'll make me answer the phone too!"

Be somebody that doesn't hide their talent...

Be the Somebody that gets it done – Be the Somebody that Everybody can depend on – Be the Somebody that when Nobody is Looking, you are still Some Body – Be the Somebody that Everybody wants to know! DO what Anybody could have done But Nobody was willing to DO! Be the leader that comes in to get fed!

Sigma Alpha Pi – I encourage you from this day forward; become the best leader that you can be!

Be the Somebody that Nobody would Doubt – That Anybody will want -And Everybody will know - you are a future Leader, with great Potential!

Sigma Alpha Pi

Congratulations on your induction into the National Society of Leadership and Success.

Chapter 1

Training or Compliance

"You only get one – Day 1"

I learned many years ago from watching the 'Wizard of Oz' that it is always best to start from the beginning. I am going to move forward at a fast pace... cautiously and make a few of assumptions.

"James, now you know what they say about assumptions..."
says the inner voice

I know, but work with me inner voice. My assumption will be if you're reading this book, you are a manager striving to become an effective leader. Which means someone saw something in you... it also means you have potential to be a great leader. Or, you may actually be a leader now and you are looking for a couple of pointers to add to your toolbox of proficiency. Or, you have hopes of being a leader and you are filling your toolbox with any and everything you can get a hold of... You plan to use discernment to make the right choices for when you need to make leadership decisions. *(tear, tear)* Or, you may be reading this book to be overly critical of everything that I have written.

"You are a manager, go to another book"
says the inner voice

This book is for those that understand to become an effective leader you have to study, read, and reach for anything that may help you. You have to understand your people and know your processes. The beautiful thing about knowledge is that you can never get enough of it. I have learned from everyone I have come into contact with; yes, that means sometimes you learn what not to do to be successful.

You will hear me say "the beautiful thing" throughout this book. Because leading people to success is a beautiful thing.

Day 1

As a leader you have to set the tone from Day 1 – Which means before you address your 'New Team' you have to do your research. You were put in place because you know your job. If you take over a successful team you will have to do a temperature check to see if the team is deflated from getting a new boss. You want to lean on the team to learn about the processes that have been effective. Their former boss was promoted because of the success of the team.

"Don't change for change sake." ~ Jamesism
I have had success managing multiple teams and most teams I have taken over to supervise were not doing

well. When the team finally gets on the right track and start producing at a high level it is because the processes align with the mentorship. The mentorship equates to ownership of the process. Ironically, each time I was promoted the person that took over after me was let go or moved on for one reason or another. The team that was turned around, energetic, and motivated, was deflated and not producing. When you "change for change sake." you mess with camaraderie and your acceptance as a leader.

When Phil Jackson took over the Bulls and the Lakers, they won multiple championships. Yes, he had great players but he was also a great coach. He fused a team together and put them on the same page. Now I'm no Phil Jackson, well maybe a little... But the tone for success was set from day one!

If you take over a non-producing team, you don't have to go through employee records to find out who the weak links are; chances are if you got the promotion the manager that left the nonproducing team was the weak link. Which means the former manager probably has multiple people written up with one foot out the door? You cannot fall victim to what was left in your hands.

The beautiful thing is you have a 'New Team' – they all feel they have been given new life so if you approach it RIGHT – and not like they are useless, you won't lose that 'new car smell' the moment you open the door.

Effective leaders do not go into a situation with a mindset to get rid of the people they have been entrusted to mentor and improve. You were hired to turn things around. Your job is to mentor people and manage processes.

> *I remember when I took over a team a couple of years ago and I was directed to write one of my subordinates' up for not meeting quarterly expectations. The day I started as the new manager, I was the bad guy. I had a group of people running around scared. How can you follow a leader you don't trust? How can you follow a leader that you believe works for "HQ"? A "YES MAN" ~ being a novice I did what I was told ~ here I was with a new team that couldn't trust me- They figured I would manage them to success with the same failed principles of the manager before me. Hindsight being 20/20, I should have pushed back.*

> **When you set the tone you take ownership for every failure and every success!**

When you set the tone you take ownership for every failure and every success that the team has achieved or didn't achieve before you got there. "We" is the key phrase for success. Remember, the entire team is operating under a new slate. Granted, you may have to let some of them go down the road but an effective leader's goal is to make everyone a success under their tutelage through training and enforcing compliance. You cannot set the tone of training without the buy-in from your people. They have to view you as the expert. When you set the tone that you will not be teaching work ethic, you set the tone that states everyone is responsible for doing their job. The next thing I address is training and compliance.

"I am a stickler for training and compliance. If you need training let me know and I will provide it. No one gets a free pass and we will all operate from the same page." says the inner voice

Professional Reference #2:

James Sutton, a proven professional who understands leadership and the concept of managing teams to successful outcomes. I have had the pleasure of serving under his leadership for the last two years at ITT-Technical Institute, North Campus. Charlotte, NC and I have observed him motivate and inspire his leadership teams to levels above and beyond. He is a person to be reckoned with throughout the educational industry. He inspires his professionals to seek greatness at all levels, both in their personal and professional lives. Go Git-em Mr. Sutton.

Charles H. Witherspoon Jr.,
Witherspoon Enterprises Inc. CEO
Author / Motivational Speaker
Authored the Book "No Title to Success"

Training

You cannot teach work ethic – Please repeat this a dozen times before you move on.

"I cannot teach work ethic" says the inner voice

Too many managers approach leadership with the mindset that they can beat someone over the head with something and it will eventually work.

The sad thing is it's true. You will eventually produce something but you will also increase your work load as a manager. You will suffer from morale issues and your turnover rates will be high. As a manager, you will find yourself engrossed in the interviewing process and you will spend a lot of your time interviewing new candidates. The funny thing is you will eventually have to train the new people you hire. Imagine if you were able to train the people you have. Hmmmm

"But James they are non-productive, they don't get it." says the inner voice

Training unproductive people is a challenge which is why it is critical for you to connect with them while the "new car smell" is fresh. Once you come on board as a new leader, it they are able to sink away to their norm, it will be harder to reach them. Establishing the guidelines under your watch is critical. The New leadership guidelines will be the most important task you achieve in the first 24 hrs.

In one of my positions as Director of Admissions, I took over a team that had not met goal in a number of starts and we were coming up on our next start date. When I took over I simply stated – "I do not teach work ethic." My expectation was that everyone came to work – to work every day; giving less than 100% would not be acceptable. I wasn't mean or condescending, I was matter of fact. I honestly believe, I cannot teach work ethic. I found out later on, that some folk were a little nervous about my arrival – Some stated they didn't like me. But they understood my expectation at the door. When I arrived we were at 33% of goal and within 2 weeks not only did we meet our goal, we exceeded it.

The District Manager said "it was something short of a miracle... lol" - I wouldn't say that but I knew I had a good team and they knew I didn't teach work ethic.

Training starts with setting an expectation of excellence. Then you observe and correct on the spot. I believe in public correction and private counseling. I look at each error or concern as a training opportunity. You have to have an open dialog with your team, in an environment where they feel they have a voice. If you as the leader, continuously throw out your ideas, your thoughts, and do not listen to your team or get feedback, you will create a culture of "Yes, Men" – You will not get to the root of the ineffective processes and your team will not have a voice; that is an unhealthy environment. There is usually one of two things that affect a Leaders Success – Training or Compliance.

Observe and Correct

I know you heard me say observe and correct on the spot; in public. But you didn't stop me. I know we are from a kinder gentler mindset... some of you feel it is wrong to talk about problems or concerns in public. You may struggle because there is a secrecy overtone to your leadership process.

"James I figured you would tell us more." says the inner voice

> *There is usually one of two things that affect a Leaders Success – Training or Compliance*

Some of you may have heard the phrase "public praise and private counseling." I do not want you to confuse observe and correct with a counseling, demeaning, or chastising. When I say observe and correct, you are fixing a potential volatile situation on the spot. Too often we let negative and potentially hazardous situations fester in our work environment. You have to nip it in the bud.

I worked in an environment once with a few negative people with nasty attitudes and demeanors. It lasted all of an hour before we were in my office meeting and talking the situation over. No one wants to work with the guy that has a negative mean demeanor. I believe in calling folk out and addressing the issue. When it comes to the process it's no different.

I mean when you observe someone saying or doing something outside of the process – You don't throw them under the bus to change the oil as my subordinate would say. You ask them a question about the process. – No yelling; no demeaning! I've found when you observe and correct, other people don't make the same mistake. They were indirectly trained on the correct process. I operate with every situation being an opportunity to train.

With this being the age of technology, we have a tendency to email our way through the day. On a given day, I get over a hundred emails. When it comes to my subordinates and supervisors I have a "3 email rule". After the third email or text, we have to meet face to face; at the least phone call.

Emails and electronic communication takes on a tone of its own. It is imperative that while you set the tone, you listen to the tone of all communication around you.

Training Day

> *You cannot use a cookie-cutter training approach because people learn differently.*

I cannot overemphasize the need to go right in and establish that you do not teach work ethic. Then let people go back to work - Observe and Correct on the spot. If you do not understand a process under a new system, spend time observing that aspect of the job. Have the person you are working with explain the entire process to you. You will find that as they explain the process in the open, multiple people will chime in.

I remember when I was in the Air Force and I was the Operations Supervisor; on my initial visits to the Military Entrance Processing Station (MEPS) I would conduct inspections by having the individual explain the process. I was familiar with it but I was not the expert. And it never failed that someone would step in to correct or assist person I was talking with; it is as if they did not want their department to look bad in front of the new leader.

This happens because you are new and they are trying to impress you with the knowledge they have of the process. I've found, I learned more in the first two weeks of observation and correction then I do over the next 6 months. - One of the biggest areas of concern that I have seen in leadership is ineffective training. You cannot use a cookie-cutter training approach because people learn differently. If you want to increase your credibility as a leader demonstrate and perform at a high level. The processes must always be the same; the training must be creative and interesting. My subordinates never know what they are going to get in training, but they know it will be relevant and it will address the process.

Processes vs. Training
Processes fail through lack of execution - people fail from lack of training - Training fails from lack of application - processes fail from lack of compliance.

It's imperative that you eliminate every crutch - You have to take away excuses by not accepting any. I recently attempted to help an organization that had multiple levels of training concerns – from leadership to management - there were no processes in place - on the surface they looked good but as I worked with the organization I saw that the core of the problem was the foundation; it was broken - there was a lot of direction given but there were no processes in place. There was no cohesion - one part of the organization was not communicating with the other part of the organization – The leadership in place were concerned with their own departments instead of the big picture – The CEO did not effectively communicate the process and vision to the of rest of the leadership team and the organization.

I stepped away from that organization because leaders have to seek help; like mentors leaders have to want to see change. I tell my subordinates all the time that I can't want it more than them. As I look at the organization from a distance, they have progressed but it has been slow due to lack of processes – As a leader, you have to identify those that can assist you and those that have a heart for the business. Beyond both those attributes, they have to have the experience and qualifications. One concern I have seen through the years, new leaders promote or show favoritism for unproved and unqualified people. Just because I like someone does not mean they should be put in leadership. As a leader look at people that have put time in the organization; take a hard look at their

desire and will to work. Don't play favoritism –
Everyone must work to the same level of expectation.

*"You cannot replace experience and wisdom with
arrogance and envy then expect to move forward.
When someone with experience and wisdom takes the
time to bless you with some attention simply because
they care about your journey, be quiet and listen. Get
the knowledge, apply it, and move forward. ~ Eric
Brice, Musician-Vocalist*

Favoritism

Favoritism is a trap.
The worst thing you
can do as a leader is to
give the perception of

> *New leaders promote or
> show favoritism for
> unproved and
> unqualified people.*

favoritism. Real or Perceived favoritism can have a
devastating effect on team morale. It's the leader's
responsibility to eliminate the perception and reality
of favoritism. It starts by the leader holding everyone
accountable to the same standard. Later in the book
we will discuss star performers and volunteers; you
will see the reasons why both star performers and
volunteers must be held to the same standard as
everyone else.

A sure fire way for a leader to eliminate the perception
of favoritism is to manage effective processes. This
requires managers to hold everyone accountable to the
same process.

When I served as the Director of Admissions – I had one of the best recruiters I ever come across in my life. She was phenomenal – Her best year she enrolled 151 students against a goal of 100. I had other top performers and everyone would think that she was being fed leads. She was just great. I held her to the same standard as everyone else - For the rest of the team that was huge because they knew no matter what level you performed on, you were held to the same standard.

When you hold everyone to the same standard the work environment is a little more pleasant. If we

> *It starts by the leader holding everyone accountable to the same standard.*

find there is a better way to do something then everybody needs to do it that way. Some will try to complicate leadership by stating it cannot be applied in every industry; that's just not true. I understand there will be different cultures within the organization however; there should not be different processes between one person and another. Ineffective processes should not prohibit effective leadership.

Rules, Guidelines, and Standards

The rules associated with your process are the rights and wrongs -the yes and no – of the standard. Effective leaders do not operate in the grey area. If your team doubts your moral standard, they will question your integrity.

Our subordinates use the Guidelines associated with the rules to complete assigned task - while the rules have no grey area - guidelines are typically one's interpretation of the

> *Effective leaders do not operate in the grey area.*

rules - this is where effective leaders have an opportunity to increase effectiveness - enforcement of and working within the standard is what makes compliance enforcement a continuous challenge – understand the guidelines are also where your people are allowed a level of creativity to get the job done – this is where you find the process improvements and best practices; as a leader I often remind my subordinates that there is no grey area - if there is a question about a process or if they feel as if something is borderline - as Nike says "Just <u>don't</u> do it"

"James Nike says Just Do It!" says the inner voice

Compliance is having a total understanding of how your people operate within the system; within the rules, guidelines, and standard- with the mindset of excellence.

"Why are the rules so simple James ?"
says the inner voice

Everyone works in a production environment! - When you go to work you are expected to get something done, you are expected to produce results. Your expectation as a leader is to ensure your people are being productive. Period!

Trying ain't producing - trying is trying - if what you are trying doesn't work - try something else –
Produce! Just make sure before you make a change that the change is measurable within a process.

> When you go to work you are expected to get something done.

"James you have not talked much about the process."
says the inner voice

Inner Voice I had to plant seeds - I just heard someone preach at our church and he talked about planting seeds.

The Process

I cannot over emphasize the importance of having processes and procedures in place for your organization and department.

"Where there is no vision, the people perish."
--Proverbs 29:18

When we have rules, guidelines, and standards incorporated in an organized system - we have a process. Where there is no process production is challenged. Established procedures allows a manager to evaluate where you they are broke - you can then make a leadership decision based on the data received - I worked for a CEO whose mantra was "you are not smarter than the data" - while I agree, I will add that "the data cannot be smarter than you." With proper processes one is able to take the data to interpret shortfalls and act accordingly - remember before you go off on your subordinates about noncompliance revisit the Training and Compliance mindset - now you can take the appropriate action.

I had to release people from their position for lack of production – I never had anyone mad at me. They understood because they knew I trained and provided the necessary feedback for them to be successful. Unfortunately, everyone can't do every job. But they left knowing they were given every opportunity to succeed. Don't use corrective action as punishment – Use it as a tool to correct. If it don't work out you know you did your best to prepare the people under you tutelage. While they may not have made it in your organization. You mentored a future leader that will use your training techniques to help someone else. Your other subordinates are watching. If you are holding everyone accountable, they will produce at a higher level.

Leaders Don't Panic

As a leader, you have to keep it together. You can't panic and make rash decisions without giving the situation thought. There will be decisions that have to be made on the spot, but if you have effective processes in place that decision is not off the cuff; it's based on the processes that have been implemented.

When a situation arises that requires your attention, take the time to evaluate the situation based on the data and the facts, not on the rumor and innuendo. If it has not been validated it is hearsay. Innuendo is like a sarcastic plague; it takes on a life of its own. All too often a leader makes a decision based on hearsay then pride prevents them from correcting the situation.

"Secret... as a leader, people will talk about you behind your back, get them to say good things" says the inner voice.

Yes! As a leader, people will talk about you. To be an effective leader, you have to brush that off, base your decision on the facts. Listen, chances are, if you heard about them talking behind your back – think about how it got back to you. If it came from another source, that source was talking about you too. If folk are talking about you, they are listening to you. If they are listening, even if they are complaining about the process, the beautiful thing is they are listening. Unless they are talking about doing harm to you and your family, the talk doesn't matter; the data of the process does.

Don't panic and fire them or drive them away. If it means that much to them to talk about the situation behind your back, it means they are vested. Go to them, talk to them directly, and listen. People are your greatest asset – People with concerns are your best asset because they will tell you the truth out of frustration... if you let them. Listen! Don't judge and be critical without the facts. Don't panic! Hearing the truth will help you move forward. Your "Yes Men" will smile and grin. Your sore people will tell the truth. Listen to them!

Their perception is their reality and chances are they are not the only ones that feel that way. They are not the only ones talking. They are the only ones that got "caught" talking about it.

Matthew 18:15-20 MSG

[15-17] "If a fellow believer hurts you, go and tell him—work it out between the two of you. If he listens, you've made a friend. If he won't listen, take one or two others along so that the presence of witnesses will keep things honest, and try again. If he still won't listen, tell the church. If he won't listen to the church, you'll have to start over from scratch, confront him with the need for repentance, and offer again God's forgiving love.

Everyone's opinions matter – sometimes you have to hear the cons to improve the pros. If their concern has no validity chances are there was a breakdown in communication. The beautiful thing is that gives you the opportunity to train and share the vision.

As a leader, you have to assess a situation based on the facts. When you make decisions based on your emotions, not only are you acting out of hurt, you are hurting people. Real talk!

Professional Reference #3:

I had the pleasure of working with James at ITT-Technical Institute for over a year. James was always very professional and polite even when he was breaking the ice with a joke at meetings. His dedication to not only the student body, but to the overall education received at the school was very present. He always makes his positive presence on the campus known either by his pop-ins to the classes to announce something, or his willingness to take a pie in the face for a good cause. I have met few people like James Sutton, and I learned a lot from him as a professional and how to be a professional

Justin Worsham
Tier 3 JDA Support at Boy Scouts of America

Earned Respect vs. Given Respect
In the military, it is evident from the stripes on our uniforms who is in charge. However, we had given respect based on our rank and earned respect based on our leadership ability. In my 23 years of service, I

found that the earned respect always outweighed the given respect.

Every time I hear someone in leadership use their title or position as a precursor to their statement such as, "I'm the Chief, I'm the CEO, or because I am in charge," they lose credibility and respect with me. If you are in charge, you shouldn't have to announce it. If you feel a need to continuously announce that you are the CEO, do a checkup from the neck-up, do you have your people's respect. Are you truly a leader? You need to look to see who is following you. I will also like to point out that it is not your rank, status, title, or level of education and/or your level of experience that gets people to work for you. It's your leadership ability.

> *I found that the earned respect always outweighed the given respect.*

Now don't get me wrong I value education – But the reality is the education is only confirmation that you studied a particular subject; it does not mean you learned how to apply it. It takes practice, study, and application to become an effective leader. Too often I see people pushed into leadership roles without any experience, formal training or guidance. If you are the CEO... train and mentor your people before you send them to the wolves.

I was an effective leader before I had my H.S. Diploma.

I went to John Jay H.S. in Brooklyn NY. My senior year I was voted in as class president. Mind you I was a straight D student in High School but I was popular. (pick up my other book for the story) Long story – short – I was faced with encouraging and leading a student body in the midst of a paper shortage. This meant that we would have no yearbook. I rallied the troops at an assembly and we got our year book. It wasn't my credentials – It was my ability to motivate and encourage people into action. If you see a need, make sure the need is for the good of the organization. I've seen amazing things accomplished with a team on the same page. "

In the military and at the office, you want your troops to respect you in and out of uniform. When you earn respect, your troops will literally die for you, because they know you will die for them.

Professional Reference #4:

MSgt Sutton was one of the best NCO's I have ever come across. His professionalism and leadership ability has surpassed any that I have known. He has the uncanny ability to connect, train, and discipline his airmen all in the same breath. MSgt Sutton's sense of humor is one of his strongest attributes. He doesn't make light of a situation – He just eliminates the pressure and focuses on the problem. I thoroughly enjoyed working with MSgt Sutton.

Jennifer Bacon., Captain
US Air Force

Chapter 1 – Wow, RECAP!!!

This is really all you need – Trust me!

"Trust you? James – did you really say "trust me"? says the inner voice

Look, implement these steps as a part of your regular routine – change your mind set in regard to leadership; Try the lessons of Volume One

All you need to know to make it at the next level:

Training or Compliance

Training is the glue that holds a team together – It requires creativity and passion.

1. What approach should you take toward training and compliance?

_____

_____

_____

2. Which is more important; Training or Compliance?

_____

_____

_____

The Beautiful Thing

Your new team is ready and willing; able?

3. Why is having a "New Team" a beautiful thing?

_____

_____

_____

4. How should you approach your new team?

_____

_____

_____

Don't Teach Work Ethic

Don't do it! If you pacify you lose!

5. Why is teaching work ethic not a proper way to lead?

_____

_____

_____

6. What actions can you take to establish control at the door?

_____

_____

_____

Observe and Correct

On the spot! Don't let problems fester! Enforce the "3 email rule" – set the tone!

7. Why is it important to correct or address concerns immediately?

_____

_____

8. How should your public correction be reinforced?

_____

_____

_____

Processes & Training

Train your people on the processes in place. Everyone should operate with the same tools using the same rules.

9. Your process is how you do business; does your team know the process?

_____

_____

Favoritism

Be fair!

10. Why should you NOT show favoritism?

_____

_____

Leaders Don't Panic

As a leader, you have to assess a situation based on the facts. When you make decisions based on your emotions, not only are you acting out of hurt, you are hurting people.

11. Why should you avoid making decisions on the spot?

_____

_____

12. How does rumors and innuendo affect your decisions?

_____

_____

Earned & Given Respect

The respect you earn will take you further than any title you receive. It's not about being right or being liked; it's about being fair.

13. Is earned respect or given respect most important?

_____

_____

14. Do you feel you have your team's respect?

_____

_____

Final Thoughts for this chapter

If you noticed, I have not addressed mentorship in this first chapter. However, if you work on some of the discussed practices, you have already begun the mentoring process. You are touching your people in a way that your earned respect stock will rise. It is critical that the processes be in place before the mentorship takes hold. You can only mentor people to the effectiveness of the process.

Future Volumes and Chapters will be released upon completion. Please 'like' my Facebook page at Career Rehabilitation. If you have questions about anything discussed – Please email me at lookatyourboss@gmail.com

P.S.

I may never get to the other volumes of this book because then this would be a long book and you would read it... soooo.... I left you a few nuggets about what the chapters would look like.

Don't forget to 'Like" my Facebook page

Career Rehabilitation

Volume 2

Chapter 2

Motivation & Accountability

"The beautiful thing"

Motivation is directly in line with accountability. To get the most from your people you have to have the ability to motivate them and have the guts to hold them accountable. If they leave because of accountability then they were not a good fit. You can't teach work ethic but you can be organized.

I believe in the 10,000 Steps-A-Day to Leadership mindset is the best way to emphasize the "Inspect What you Expect" Mantra. To hold people accountable they have to know your looking. If you're not looking then you are not following up. Some jobs require micromanaging the details and other jobs require micromanaging the process. At no time as a manager should you allow things to happen without your knowledge of what is going on; even with your best supervisors. Checking in and diving in are the natural progressions of management.

Motivation

Some would say that the motivation is the fact that you have a job. That's the Blessing! However, it is not the motivation. If you follow sports that have this person called the coach. You might say a million dollar athlete doesn't need coaching or motivation because they are million dollar athletes. For most of us that would be motivation enough... so we say.

'that would definitely motivate me" says the inner voice.

Sure inner voice. That's what I thought. Now I don't make millions but as a thousanaire, I thought as my salary increased my motivation would but it wasn't all about the money.

"really?!?" says the inner voice.

Matthew 20:16 NIV

[16] "So the last will be first, and the first will be last."

Volume 3

Chapter 3

Follow-up & Follow-Through

"Not my problem or my concern"

If you have been around me for any length of time, you have heard my catch phrase. "Not my problem or my concern." The follow-up and follow-through is a simple concept. You have to follow-up after you put out guidance, instructor, and training. This is where the 'no excuses" mindset comes in to play – If you make more excuses then reasons to get the job done, you are finding ways not to be successful. That's not my problem or my concern!

---

1 Peter 5:2 NIV

[2] Be shepherds of God's flock that is under your care, watching over them—not because you must, but because you are willing, as God wants you to be; not pursuing dishonest gain, but eager to serve;

Volume 4

Chapter 4

Star Performers & Volunteers

"Equal is as equal does..." Forrest Gump

I have seen more problems and concerns with leaders giving preferential treatment to "star performers" and volunteers. There is only one standard and everyone has to adhere to it. If a volunteer has a concern with the process they are simply not a good fit for the position. Preferential treatment and adjusting the process for one person causes problems immediately and long term.

Hebrews 13:17 NIV

[17] Have confidence in your leaders and submit to their authority, because they keep watch over you as those who must give an account. Do this so that their work will be a joy, not a burden, for that would be of no benefit to you.

Volume 5

Chapter 5

Implementation vs. Daily Frustration

"Do it now or suffer later"

If you do not implement processes you open the door for continued concerns and problems daily. While implementation will be painful for some, once the process is online, it will benefit everyone. It is imperative that you explain the process before implementation to avoid information overload.

Galatians 6:9 NIV

[9] Let us not become weary in doing good, for at the proper time we will reap a harvest if we do not give up.

Volume 6

Chapter 6

Mentorship

"Training or Compliance"

Mentorship is basically taking everyone under your wing and stretching their abilities beyond where they see themselves. This comes from training and compliance. Leadership can't be taught it can only be learned!

---

1 Timothy 5:17 NIV

[17] The elders who direct the affairs of the church well are worthy of double honor, especially those whose work is preaching and teaching.

Volume 7

Chapter 7

Management

"Processes make the world go round"

Effective processes must be in place to effectively mentor people. As a manager, it is your job and responsibility to make sure the process works. You have to manage the process. If the process is broken or not in place you limit the potential of your people. You can only effectively mentor to the level of the process. You create an environment of frustration when leaders are forced to make decisions when no guidance or process is in place; you create an environment where everyone is operating differently, trying to achieve the same goal. You may get there, but the level of frustration will be there first; and when you get there the frustration of poor processes shows.

Corinthians 14:33 NIV

[33] For God is not a God of disorder but of peace—as in all the congregations of the Lord's people.

Volume 8

Chapter 8

People & Processes

"Mentor & Manage"

When we put it all together, it comes down to mentoring people and monitoring processes. No one wants to fail. But we create an environment of failure as leaders when we do not have our stuff together. You have to plan your work and work your plan according with effective processes and motivated people. I hear too often that processes are not needed. I see the opposite when I work with organizations that lack processes. The people are willing but often time frustrated and angry.

Romans 13:1 NIV

13 Let everyone be subject to the governing authorities, for there is no authority except that which God has established. The authorities that exist have been established by God.

Volume 9

Chapter 9

You are a Leader

"Lead by Example"

At the end of the day –Who will your people say you are as a leader? Are you a good motivator and a poor manager? Delegate! If you're a good manager and poor leader – delegate! At the end of the day if you do not identify your weaknesses, you will have many frustrated people around that want to help, but feel it's better to leave. Mentor people and Manage Processes; It really is that simple.

John 13: 13-17 NIV

13 "You call me 'Teacher' and 'Lord,' and rightly so, for that is what I am. 14 Now that I, your Lord and Teacher, have washed your feet, you also should wash one another's feet. 15 I have set you an example that you should do as I have done for you. 16 I tell you the truth, no servant is greater than his master, nor is a messenger greater than the one who sent him. 17 Now that you know these things, you will be blessed if you do them.

Made in the USA
Middletown, DE
30 April 2015